Take it All

Take it All

By
Rod Parsley

Columbus, Ohio

TAKE IT ALL

Printed in the United States of America.
ISBN 1-880244-87-X

Published by:

Results Publishing
World Harvest Church
P.O. Box 32932
Columbus, Ohio 43232

Unless otherwise noted, all Scripture references are from the King James Version of the Bible.

TABLE OF CONTENTS

Introduction

THE POWER TO TAKE IT ALL

Two men crouched on the outskirts of Canaan staring at the city of Jericho. They took note of all the entrances to the city. They calculated the number of guards at the entrance of each gate. They were sent on a mission by Moses along with ten other men.

> And Moses sent them to spy out the land of Canaan, and said unto them, Get you up this way southward, and go up into the mountain: And see the land, what it is; and the people that dwelleth therein, whether they be strong or weak, few or many. And be of good courage, and bring of the fruit of the land. Now the time was the time of the firstripe grapes (Numbers 13:17, 18 and 20b).

The stories of this vast countryside began flooding the mind of Joshua, one of the twelve spies. Jehovah said it was a land flowing with milk and honey, of rivers and valleys, a place which drank from the rains of heaven. The landscape was much more beautiful and luxurious than Joshua had ever imagined. There was only one problem.

The land was populated by giants.

To Joshua and his companion Caleb, this was just a small obstacle compared to the glorious rewards of the land. But there was a rumbling among the other ten spies.

They did not like the looks of these heathen people. They felt threatened, discouraged, and defeated even before there was to be a battle. They even began to compare themselves to grasshoppers.

How could they fight such a formidable foe? Their hearts began to melt within them and there was even talk of a revolt against Moses for leading them into the dry, barren wilderness. Certainly, they would have been better off as slaves bearing the burden of their former Egyptian taskmasters. So in unison they decided to tell Moses the news—victory was impossible and Canaan would never belong to them. This proved to be one of the greatest tactical errors of Israel. The ten spies sealed their fate and the fate of the majority of their family and friends with the advice they were about to give.

The ten spies' treasonous words became a blight to the entire nation of Israel. They instilled fear in the hearts of the people and the end result was a forty year sentence—one year for each day that the spies searched the land—handed down by God.

For forty years the Israelites were doomed to wander in the barren wilderness with the Promised Land still in full view. For forty years the generation that despised God and His Word began to slowly die off.

God's promise had not changed. He still desired for the children of Israel to come into their full possession and take all the land of Canaan. The harvest waited while the next generation grew up and began to embrace the promise the Lord had made many years ago.

During their incarceration in the wilderness, under the tutelage of Moses, God began to turn the once-spy, Joshua, into the future leader of Israel. At the death of Moses, the Lord spoke:

> Moses my servant is dead; now therefore arise, go over this Jordan, thou, and all this people, unto the land which I do give to them, even to the children of Israel. Every place that the sole of your foot shall tread upon, that have I given unto you, as I said unto Moses (Joshua 1:2, 3).

Though God's servant had died, His promise was still alive. That promise belonged to a new generation of Israelites and His blessing, every place that the sole of their foot touched, was about to be theirs.

The time had come to take it all.

The Miracle of the Resurrection Seed

For twenty years, the word of the Lord to all our partners and friends that are connected to this ministry has never changed. I believe a vital part of fulfilling God's promise and taking all of your harvest goes back to a revelation He gave me early in my ministry. It was twenty years ago that the Lord gave me a word which astounded me. He said, "One time a year during Easter I want you to celebrate Me giving My best through My Son Jesus by you giving your best and sowing one week's income." Every year miracles have multiplied in the lives of the people who have received this word as their own.

In 2003, God called us to stand "one for all and all for one" in the great fight of faith to possess our land of promise and bring Jesus Christ, our Savior, the reward of His suffering. But now in 2004, with the flaming finger of the Holy Ghost, I believe God wants to engrave His Word on the fleshly tablets of your heart. You will no longer just be a spectator of the Word. You will not just be a fan of its message. I believe in 2004 God is preparing to pour out a fresh anointing and give us the power to take back our cities, our families, our peace, our joy, our finances—to take it all with the power of a risen Savior.

This message of the Resurrection Seed has reverberated around the world in the lives of God's people, as countless men and women have stood united in their faith in obedience to His Word. Yet over the years some people have tried to get me to change this message. Others have tried to get me to stop preaching it altogether. Every year God has been faithful to fulfill His promise to those who receive this revelation and make it their own. The anointing is upon the truth of the Resurrection Seed and it has stood the test of time. This word has not changed. This year as you are faithful to hear and obey that word, I believe God is going to pour out His Spirit in even greater measure to empower you with a fresh anointing to "take it all."

Deuteronomy 8:18 declares, " But thou shalt remember the Lord thy God: for it is he that giveth thee power to get wealth, that he may establish his covenant which he sware unto thy fathers, as it is this day." God wants us to establish His covenant of blessing in the earth, but we need the finances in order to do it.

I believe this vision of the Resurrection Seed will not only be a revelation to your spirit, but it will become an impartation whereby you will be able to reap all the blessings the Lord has for you. The Bible says, "The steps of a good man are ordered by the Lord: and he delighteth in his way" (Psalm 37:23). In other words when you pick your feet up, God places them in the direction He wants you to go.

If you have picked up this book, I believe you are reading it by divine appointment. In its pages you will learn the power available to you to possess your promised harvest and take everything that belongs to you. God has a plan for you, and part of that plan is to impart this revelation into your spirit. It is my prayer that you receive this vital truth because God wants you to experience His supernatural blessing in your home. He wants you to manifest the miracle of Resurrection Seed in your family. He wants you to see your loved ones come to the saving grace of our Lord and Savior, Jesus Christ.

Israel had a word for forty years but the first generation couldn't receive it. It was the final generation that God appointed to take it all. I believe in 2004 you have been called to the kingdom for such a time as this.

There are still enemies ahead and total occupation of your harvest will not come without a fight. Remember, to the victor goes the spoils.

Your harvest is here and it is time to take it all.

Chapter 1

GOING HOME

> Be strong and of a good courage: for unto this people shalt thou divide for an inheritance the land, which I sware unto their fathers to give them (Joshua 1:6).

What is it that causes the compulsion to get where we are going? What is it that causes men to forge forward through the deepest darkness or driest deserts to get to their destination? This struggle can be summarized in one simple statement: it's all about going home.

Our ancient ancestors, the Israelites, were a group of wayfaring wanderers, traveling through the trackless waste of a treacherous wilderness on their way to a home none of them had ever seen.

> For the Lord thy God bringeth thee into a good land, a land of brooks of water, of fountains and depths that spring out of valleys and hills; A land of wheat, and barley, and vines, and fig trees, and pomegranates; a land of oil olive, and honey; A land wherein thou shalt eat bread without scarceness, thou shalt not lack any thing in it; a land whose stones are iron, and out of whose hills thou mayest dig brass. When thou hast eaten and art full, then thou shalt bless the Lord thy God for the good land which he hath given thee (Deuteronomy 8:7-10).

From the suffering and slavery of Egypt through the sojourning and solitude of the wilderness, they stood on the precipice of the satisfaction and sufficiency of the Promised Land. Sustained by El Shaddai in the Sinai Desert, this chosen people had crossed the river Jordan and stood as the conquerors of Jericho and Ai.

Ancient Israel's inheritance was a Promised Land. Ours is a Land of Promise. We are compelled by spiritual instincts acting as a divine honing device, and our objective is nothing less than total occupation and possession of that promise. We must possess our promise because there are grapes we haven't tasted, fields we haven't harvested, and houses we haven't lived in. There are signs we haven't seen, wonders we haven't witnessed, and miracles that haven't manifested yet.

It's Harvest Time

God wants us to take all of the harvest He has prepared for us in our Promised Land. However, we must remember that there is a parallel of the contradiction between the victory at Jericho and the defeat at Ai. God doesn't want us to bypass our Ai because that is where our spoils await. He wants us to go all the way to the victory side.

In order for Israel to receive their harvest, they had to first cross over the Jordan River from the wilderness into the land of Canaan. It is important to note the time at which God had them pass over. The Book of Joshua records:

> And it came to pass, when the people removed from their tents, to pass over Jordan, and the priests bearing the ark of the covenant before the people;

> And as they that bare the ark were come unto Jordan, and the feet of the priests that bark the ark were dipped in the brim of the water, (for Jordan overfloweth all his banks all the time of harvest,) That the waters which came down from above stood and rose up upon an heap very far from the city Adam, that is beside Zaretan: and those that came down toward the sea of the plain, even the salt sea, failed, and were cut off: and the people passed over right against Jericho.
>
> And the priests that bare the ark of the covenant of the Lord stood firm on dry ground in the midst of Jordan, and all the Israelites passed over on dry ground, until all the people were passed clean over Jordan (3:14-17).

Just like the Israelites passed over the Jordan at the time of harvest, in 2004 I believe it is harvest time for people to come into the kingdom of God. Not only that, it's time for the kingdom to come into the people of God!

It is time for you take all God's kingdom has to offer and to harvest healing, victory, joy, wealth, and anointing. It's harvest time! You have prayed long enough, hoped long enough, believed long enough, tithed long enough, given long enough! It's harvest time!

That is why God doesn't just want to take you out of Egypt but He wants to take you all the way into the land of Canaan. God's promise is ultimate victory through faith in His Name. He made a similar promise many years ago to the Israelites as they drew near to their promised land. Yet for God's people as well as for you there are going to be some giants to fight along the way.

There Are Giants in the Land

Although Canaan was a land flowing with milk and honey, it was not unoccupied. It was populated by seven tribes of people who had lived there for hundreds of years. They weren't going to pack up and depart peacefully just because Israel wanted to move in. They would have to be driven out by force. Joshua declared:

> Hereby ye shall know that the living God is among you, and that he will without fail drive out from before you the Canaanites, and the Hittites, and the Hivites, and the Perizzites, and the Girgashites, and the Amorites, and the Jebusites (3:10).

You may have come to the border of your land of promise only to find it already occupied as well. The Canaanites have all been destroyed, but what they represent has endured down through the ages. Today you can place your confidence in the same God that delivered Israel.

Sickness, economic woes, and the specter of international terrorism threaten our safety, security, and sense of purpose. We can face these adversaries, however, with the same confidence that Joshua and the children of Israel had as they stormed the gates of their enemies and achieved unprecedented conquest.

God wants you to embark on a journey all the way into your promised land. I believe He has strategically positioned you before your greatest adversary. Yet you can rest assured that the greatest victory always comes at the point of your greatest battle.

Regardless of the opposition you may have encountered along the way to the promises of God, He has already paved the way to your victory in His word. As you read this book, I believe you can build your faith for the journey, as the Lord leads you into your land of blessings and abundance. But to go forward, we must sometimes look back.

Let me call your attention to one of the first groups to clash with Israel in Canaan. They were the Hivites.

> And they went to Joshua unto the camp at Gilgal, and said unto him, and to the men of Israel, We be come from a far country: now therefore make a league with us. And men of Israel said unto the Hivites, Peradverture ye dwell among us; and how shall we make a league with you?
>
> And it came to pass at the end of three days after they had made a league with them, that they heard that they were their neighbours, and that they dwelt among them (Joshua 9:6, 7, 16).

The Hivites appeared shortly after the conquest of Jericho and the eventual defeat of Ai, and they represent the enemies that want to devour your financial stabilities.

The devil's purpose is threefold—to steal, to kill, and to destroy. Jesus revealed his diabolical plan in the Book of John when He said these words:

> The thief cometh not, but for to steal, and to kill, and to destroy: I am come that they might have life, and that they might have it more abundantly (10:10).

One of the areas Satan wants to steal is your wealth, thus keeping you from being able to finance the preaching of the Gospel.

You may be thinking, "Well, I don't have anything to worry about concerning wealth, because I don't have any." No doubt the children of Israel may have said the same thing as they crossed the Jordan River. But God's plan was to give them all the wealth of the Canaanites.

They may have been a nation of wilderness wanderers, but God was turning them into a nation of Canaan land conquerors. Whatever the wicked had laid up in store was going to be transferred to the hands of the righteous.

The Bible records, "Only the cattle and the spoil of that city Israel took for a prey unto themselves, according to the word of the LORD which he commanded Joshua."

All the silver and gold, all the flocks and herds, all the treasure of every Canaanite in the city of Ai, was to be given to the children of Israel to use, to keep, or to give away. It was theirs by the law of conquest itself. They could use it for any purpose that was within God's will for their lives and that of their families.

This is why it is doubly tragic that an Israelite named Achan fell into sin at Jericho. He didn't realize that just over the next hilltop was an entire city full of spoils. Instead of waiting patiently for the promise and purpose of God to be fulfilled, he touched what God reserved for Himself alone, and was accursed as a result.

Perhaps he thought that nobody would miss the few items he stole and hid in his tent. Maybe he was overwhelmed by the plunder all around him when the walls of Jericho fell. Perhaps he feared he would miss out on the blessing if he didn't stretch forth his hand to get his share.

Let me assure you of this: we serve a God of more than enough. Don't compromise His blessing in your life and in your family by holding onto something, which belongs to God alone. Achan held onto some silver, gold, and a new suit of clothes. If he had waited just a few days longer, he could have had an entire household of spoils.

Don't believe the lie of the Hivites. They want to cripple your effectiveness for the kingdom of God through a spirit of fear. They will cause you to compromise your convictions, and hold onto what you already have in your hand. If you will hold onto God's word instead, and release what is in your hand, He will give you more than enough to meet your needs. Instead of becoming a curse, you will become a blessing to everyone around you.

You Are Part of a Mighty Army

You may be thinking about the mountain of trouble you are facing or the heartache you have endured. Let me remind you of the plight of the Israelites. At one time, they were slaves, obeying the orders of taskmasters. They had no leader; they had no visionary.

But through a man chosen and anointed by God, named Joshua, they were transformed into a mighty conquering army—and transplanted into a land they could call their own.

The Israelites encountered many delays and detours during their forty years of wilderness wandering. Some were the result of mistakes they made, but God scheduled many of their trials to get them ready for the inheritance He had already prepared for them.

Like the Israelites, you may have received a promise from the Lord. Are you wondering why that promise has not yet become a reality? I want to encourage you not to give up and not to give in. The Bible still says, "For all the promises of God in him are yea, and in him Amen, unto the glory of God by us" (2 Corinthians 1:20). Begin to believe this is your year to overtake your adversaries and take all the spoils of victory—peace, joy, health, and overflowing abundance.

If it seems as though the obstacles facing you are insurmountable, consider this: the children of Israel had to escape the pursuing Egyptian army, navigate the Red Sea, and cross a desert wasteland where there was no water or food. They overcame division and dissention in the midst of their own ranks, and then defeated not one—but seven tribes of giants before they possessed their inheritance. Not only were they successful, but they experienced blessings they could have never foreseen at the beginning of their journey.

When God is on your side, you can out-distance an army of antagonists and pass through the waters of adversity into absolute victory. We can cross the burning desert under a cloud of His power, presence, and provision, and defeat every adversary that stands between us and our harvest.

In the upcoming chapters, I am going to share with you a principle that not only propelled Israel to victory, but can catapult you to new heights in your experience with the living God.

God's Promise Is Total Victory

There is a victory that has already been won, that you have yet to fight. The Lord told the nation of Israel in

Joshua 8:1:

> And the Lord said unto Joshua, Fear not, neither be thou dismayed: take all the people of war with thee, and arise, go up to Ai: see, I have given into thy hand the king of Ai, and his people, and his city, and his land.

You will notice that God spoke in the past tense. He already saw the victory and prophesied it. Joshua and the Israelites just had to act upon that word.

Unfortunately, there are some in the body of Christ who have left the bondages of Egypt but they haven't entered into the land of promise. They may have left sickness and disease but they have not occupied the land of divine health. They have left the shackles of poverty but have yet to possess prosperity.

Perhaps you have made the decision to leave where you were in the lowlands of flat spiritual experience but now it is the time to go and take all of the spoils of Canaan. It is time to come of out bondage and enter in to the Promised Land!

God created you for the conflict. He gave birth to you for the battle. God never intended that your life in Christ should consist of merely coexisting with the very enemies arrayed against you.

Remember, He knows no victory that has not been fought in the battle. Compromise will always take the pressure off, but the end result is a life of lack and mediocrity. God wants victory to surge through every part of your being, but He can't do it with you in dry dock.

Soldiers Enlisted in the Battle

Whatever giants are arrayed against you—a broken marriage, a broken home, a lost child, a lingering sickness—you can rest assured that you do not have to battle them alone. I want to stand in covenant with you believing God to bring a harvest of victory into your life.

That is why the message of the Resurrection Seed is so vital. Together, we can come against the forces of darkness and take what rightfully belongs to you—your peace, provision, protection, joy, and hope. It is time to take it all.

Once you cross over into your Promised Land, then you can begin to drive out the previous tenants, stake your claim, and take up residence.

In the upcoming pages, you will learn the importance of enlisting as a soldier in the battle for your harvest. As you continue to read on, you will discover the three most important weapons God gave the children of Israel to succeed against their greatest adversaries—commission, commitment, and command—in order to take all of the spoils of war.

Chapter 2

LESSONS IN LEADERSHIP

> There shall not any man be able to stand before thee all the days of thy life: as I was with Moses, so I will be with thee: I will not fail thee, nor forsake thee (Joshua 1:5).

Year after year, the Lord has been faithful to lead us ever closer to the inheritance He has already provided for those who will heed and obey His word. In 2003, the Lord showed me that although there may still be strongholds of sorrow, sickness, and lack in your land of promise, it was the year to unite "one for all and all for one" to storm the gates that stand between you and absolute victory. In 2004, the time has come to possess our promised harvest and take all of the spoils of war.

The True Test of a Leader

As I mentioned in the previous chapter, one of the weapons the Lord gave to the people of Israel was His plan —or His commission—to defeat the enemies arrayed against them throughout the land of Canaan through His servant Moses.

The true test of a leader is that he leaves behind him in other men the conviction and the will to carry on. After the death of Moses, the Lord spoke to Joshua concerning the future of His people and their Promised Land.

Under his command, God miraculously dried up the Jordan River in the middle of a flood, and they crossed over into the promised Canaan land on dry ground.

But the battles weren't over—in fact, they were just beginning.

He told him to be strong and courageous. Joshua knew that victory would not be achieved without a struggle. Yet, God's word was clear. Israel would certainly conquer their enemies if they would believe the promise of the Lord and be obedient to his commands.

Not only did Joshua receive a direct word from the Lord, he also remembered the prophetic promise given years before to Abraham, the father of his people. Genesis chapter 22, verses 17 and 18 declare:

> In blessing I will bless thee, and in multiplying I will multiply thy seed as the stars of the heaven, and as the sand which is upon the sea shore; and thy seed shall possess the gate of his enemies; And in thy seed shall all the nations of the earth be blessed; because thou hast obeyed my voice.

The Word of the Lord was also clear as to how the people of God were to drive out their enemies, as He spoke to Moses in Numbers 33:50-54:

> And the Lord spake unto Moses in the plains of Moab by Jordan near Jericho, saying, Speak unto the children of Israel, and say unto them, When ye are passed over Jordan into the land of Canaan; Then ye shall drive out all the inhabitants of the

> land from before you, and destroy all their pictures, and destroy all their molten images, and quite pluck down all their high places: And ye shall dispossess the inhabitants of the land, and dwell therein: for I have given you the land to possess it.
>
> And ye shall divide the land by lot for an inheritance among your families: and to the more ye shall give the more inheritance, and to the fewer ye shall give the less inheritance: every man's inheritance shall be in the place where his lot falleth; according to the tribes of your fathers ye shall inherit.

Now standing on the precipice of the Promised Land, their leader, Joshua, must be able to receive and adequately communicate God's Word to the people.

Lessons of a Leader

Throughout history men and women whose destinies should have been sealed by defeat, discouragement, and disappointment have confounded their critics, astonished their adversaries, and staggered so-called friends and family as they stood valiant in the victory born in the very crucible of conflict. A conflict designed to cause their ultimate demise.

Held in high regard only among the excommunicated, eccentric, and extreme these exiles of society hope against hope, believe beyond belief, and refuse to flinch in the face of adversity in order to accomplish their greatest aspirations.

Such noble men and women are not born. Rather, they are built by their battles, formed by their failures, and promoted by their persecutions. Martin Luther King, Jr. said "the ultimate measure of such a man is not where he stands in moments of comfort and convenience, but where he stands at times of challenge and controversy."

Leadership rarely wears the coat of compromise. Often a great cause arises in the midst of a nation. In that time, great men with great minds and lofty ideals come forward. Sometimes the attacks they sustain are crueler than the collision of arms. They often stand alone, misunderstood by friends and family who sometimes desert and despise them. Their challenge is often to defy public opinion in order to succeed in the task at hand. These are hard lessons that any leader must learn.

All of the great leaders have one characteristic in common: it is their willingness to unequivocally confront the major anxiety of their people in their time. This is the essence of leadership.

This is a vivid description of Joshua as the mantel of leadership was passed from Moses to him in order that he may lead God's people into the land of Canaan. Deuteronomy 31:7 proclaims:

> And Moses called unto Joshua, and said unto him in the sight of all Israel, Be strong and of good courage: for thou must go with this people unto the land which the Lord hath sworn unto their fathers to give them; and thou shalt cause them to inherit it.

Joshua Believed the Lord

Joshua believed the Lord's promise for His people. You can also stand upon His covenant just as Joshua did. God's word is still true today. It doesn't matter what enemies await you. The Lord has promised you victory and blessing as you simply obey His voice. In fact, He will be with you in the midst of every challenge; He will not leave you nor forsake you!

There are still trials to overcome and adversaries to defeat in your Land of Promise, just as there were for the children of Israel. When Joshua and the children of Israel crossed the Jordan River, the promise was in sight, and the vision was clear. They realized they had to face the great walled city of Jericho in order to possess the spoils of that city. But first, they had to march around the walls once every day for six days in succession. Then, on the seventh day, they were to march seven times around, culminating in a united shout of victory!

The processional around Jericho seemed not to make any sense to their natural minds at all, but it was God's direct order. It was around that command that the Israelites united in one accord and for one purpose.

Joshua and the Israelites subdued the enemy's troops without any fighting. They captured the city without laying siege to it and overthrew their kingdom without lengthy operations in the field.

Through obedience, their victory was assured at Jericho. But then something happened between Jericho and their next battle at the city of Ai. Their vision became distorted. You see, they lost sight of their promise from God, and God was waiting for them to be obedient in unity to His commands.

Joshua chapter 7, verses 3 through 5 records the events that unfolded:

> And they returned to Joshua, and said unto him, Let not all the people go up; but let about two or three thousand men go up and smite Ai; and make not all the people to labour thither; for they are but few. So there went up thither of the people about three thousand men: and they fled before the men of Ai. And the men of Ai smote of them about thirty and six men: for they chased them from before the gate even unto Shebarim, and smote them in the going down: wherefore the hearts of the people melted, and became as water.

Joshua had sent spies into Ai. Unfortunately, he chose to trust the words of men instead of the word of God. His position of strength was compromised when he didn't send out all his men of war to conquer Ai as God had commanded.

When we compare the victory of Jericho and the defeat of Ai, we can see that unity and obedience were the twin keys to blessing, victory, and the spoils of conflict at Jericho—while disobedience and a lack of unity at Ai brought about Israel's downfall.

Joshua and the children of Israel became divided. They lost sight of the Lord's original purpose and vision for them. After their victory at Jericho, they began to reason in their minds the best way to take the remaining cities, forgetting God's word to Joshua.

We too often try to figure out the best way to deal with our problems and to deal with our adversaries. But we must remember what the Lord spoke through the prophet

Isaiah in chapter 55, verses 8 and 9: "For my thoughts are not your thoughts, neither are your ways my ways, saith the Lord. For as the heavens are higher than the earth, so are my ways higher than your ways, and my thoughts higher than your thoughts."

God had not appointed the spies to be the final authority as to how they should conquer Ai. He had already given direction to the entire camp through his prophetic voice, Joshua. But, as the nation of Israel faced their second conquest, I believe that Joshua, God's man, failed to properly communicate the vision to his people. The result was a resounding defeat for the children of Israel.

We Need a Prophetic Voice

Proverb 29:18 declares, "Where there is no vision, the people perish: but he that keepeth the law, happy is he." The word "vision" in this verse means "prophetic utterance." It doesn't mean a good idea, or how your training tells you it should be, or what the circumstances dictate! What truly matters is what "thus saith the Lord" through the prophetic voice of the visionary.

Secondly, the word "perish" in proverbs 29:18 also translates "to cast off all restraint and run wild." In other words, where God's prophetic utterance is not clearly communicated, the people will veer off course from His divine plan. Division and disobedience keep the people from achieving God's plan of absolute victory, health, and provision.

Down through the ages, humanity has always strayed from the Lord's divine appointment and strategy when they have not caught the vision of their leader. Second

Chronicles 20:20 admonishes us to, "Believe in the Lord your God, so shall ye be established; believe his prophets, so shall ye prosper."

For many, years, we have missed this vital truth. In the Book of Romans the Apostle Paul also proclaimed:

> How then shall they call on him in whom they have not believed? And how shall they believe in him of whom they have not heard? And how shall they hear without a preacher? And how shall they preach, except they be sent? As it is written, how beautiful are the feet of them that preach the gospel of peace, and bring glad tidings of good things!
>
> But they have not all obeyed the gospel. For Esaias saith, Lord, who hath believed our report? So then faith cometh by hearing, and hearing by the word of God.

Ephesians 4:11 tells us the fivefold office is that of the apostle, prophet, evangelist, pastor, and teacher. They are to preach the Word of the Lord so that all would hear and then having heard, be able to believe in Him and His promises. This is the method God uses to give direction and vision to His people.

Once you hear God's Word concerning your situation, faith comes and obedience can then follow. You can always rest upon God's Word to you.

Don't ever trust your destiny to someone else because they will always bring you a bad report. Listen to the voice of God through His Word and His ministry office gifts and you will never fail. When you begin to question His directive for your life, remember Jesus' words in the Book of John:

> But he that entereth in by the door is the shepherd of the sheep. To him the porter openeth; and the sheep hear his voice: and he calleth his own sheep by name, and leadeth them out.
>
> And when he putteth forth his own sheep, he goeth before them, and the sheep follow him: for they know his voice. And a stranger will they not follow, but will flee from him: for they know not the voice of strangers (10:2-5).

Always remember that no matter how impossible His promise may sound, God is faithful to perform it, if you just hold on.

That's the why the vision of the Resurrection Seed God gave me twenty years ago has stood the test of time. It was a prophetic word from the Lord given to me for all those who are attached to this ministry.

God's Plan Will Always Bring Your Harvest

I believe God has sounded the charge to conquer your enemy and possess your promised harvest. It's time to take it all. If God is for you, then who can be against you?

God's desire is to lead you forward to victory! First John 5: 4 declares,

> For whatsoever is born of God overcometh the world: and this is the victory that overcometh the world, even our faith.

The Word of the Lord will literally defeat the strongholds of the enemy arrayed against you.

It doesn't matter the magnitude of your problem. God will move on your behalf when you come to Him in humble faith and obedience, believing His word!

If you have a giant of sickness, lack, or heartache in your life, I want to encourage you to hold on to the promises in God's Word. Like the Israelites, you may think your journey through the wilderness has finally come to an end. You've overcome obstacle after obstacle, and your land of promise is in sight.

But just like the children of Israel, you still have adversaries standing in your path. I want to remind you that the same God that miraculously started you on your journey will surely lead you into total victory.

I am convinced that sometimes the path that God chooses for us is not the path of least resistance, but the one with the biggest giants. God's intention is not for you to be defeated, but for you to give Him glory in your ultimate victory.

Just as God told Joshua exactly what to do to defeat Jericho, He has recorded a battle plan—a strategy, if you will—for you to follow in conquering your greatest adversaries. It's always wrapped up in a word from the Lord.

Taking the Next Step

Once Joshua received God's direction for the children of Israel, it was his responsibility to take the next step to unite the people around this word. As we will see in the upcoming chapter, when Israel first went out to battle against Ai they failed miserably. Now they must regroup and recommit all of their efforts to the battle before them. It was time to take it all.

Chapter 3

COMMITMENT OR CONTENTMENT?

> And ye shall compass the city, all ye men of war (Joshua 6:3).

> Let not all the people go up; but let about two or three thousand men go up and smite Ai (Joshua 7:3).

In 2004, I believe God is sounding the charge for you to possess your promised land and take all of the harvest of blessing God has set out for you.

When the armies of Israel encamped on the banks of the Jordan River, they faced an unusual dilemma. Two tribes, Reuben and Gad, had found the land of Gilead to be ideal for raising flocks and herds. Numbers 32:1, 2, 4-6 records:

> Now the children of Reuben and the children of Gad had a very great multitude of cattle, and when they saw the land of Jazer, and the land of Gilead, that, behold, the place was a place for cattle; The children of Gad and the children of Reuben came and spake unto Moses, and to Eleazar the priest, and unto the princes of the congregation saying,

> Even the country which the Lord smote before the

> congregation of Israel, is a land for cattle, and thy servants have cattle: Wherefore, said they, if we have found grace in thy sight, let this land be given unto thy servants for a possession, and bring us not over Jordan.
>
> And Moses said unto the children of Gad and to the children of Reuben, Shall your brethren go to war, and shall ye sit here?

Reuben and Gad wanted to occupy land where they were camped. However, Moses wouldn't allow them. Why? Because he knew that a divided people cannot conquer its enemies.

It was only after Reuben and Gad made a solemn promise that they would fight alongside their brothers that Moses granted their request.

This was an important strategy that would lead to victory after victory every time it was deployed: everyone stays together; everyone moves out together, everyone fights together, and therefore everyone wins together.

In order for you to overcome your adversaries and occupy the territory the Lord has prepared just for you, it is critical that you be in agreement with God and with other believers.

The story of Joshua and the battle of Jericho is perhaps one of the best known in the entire Bible. But as great as that victory was, there were still other battles to be fought.

The next city to be conquered was a relatively minor one, called Ai. After such a complete victory over such a fearsome enemy as Jericho, the children of Israel were confident they would overthrow Ai easily. However, instead of an easy victory, they met with devastating defeat.

Committed to the Cause

There were three reasons why Israel was beaten at Ai. First, Joshua didn't clearly communicate the vision. Second, the camp was again divided. Not all the people were involved in their attempt to take the city. In other words, not all the people were involved as they were at Jericho. And third, there was sin in the camp.

In this chapter I want to focus for on the second reason. Joshua didn't send all the men to Ai, only a small number. In Joshua 6:1-3, the Lord said:

> Now Jericho was straitly shut up because of the children of Israel: none went out, and none came in. And the Lord said unto Joshua, See, I have given into thine hand Jericho; and the king thereof, and the mighty men of valour. And ye shall compass the city, all ye men of war.

When the Israelites faced the walled city of Jericho, they all marched around its walls. The directive was clear and there were no acceptable excuses to stay at home.

For six days God's people marched in unison. For six days the silence of six million Jews was itself deafening as they encompassed the city in a spirit of unity. In a show of unity with one accord they obeyed the voice of their Commander-in-Chief, Joshua.

This was a vital key to victory in Joshua's day, and is still a strategic key to victory today: everyone has to get involved. Everyone goes into battle together.

From the precedent set by Moses, and the instructions given by God, all the men of war certainly should have been sent into the second conflict at Ai and involved in the battle instead of just a few. They lacked commitment to the cause and became content with their victory at Jericho. Notice what happened. The Bible records:

> And Joshua sent men from Jericho to Ai, which is beside Bethaven, on the east side of Bethel, and spake unto them, saying, Go up and view the country. And the men went up and viewed Ai. And they returned to Joshua, and said unto him, Let not all the people go up; but let about two or three thousand men go up and smite Ai; and make not all the people to labour thither; for they are but few. So there went up thither of the people about three thousand men: and they fled before the men of Ai (Joshua 7:2-4).

It is so easy to forget from where God has brought us. After one successful conflict, the Israelites felt they were experienced in the art of war. They began to rely upon their own ability to defeat their enemy. They failed to remember that it was Jehovah who had drown the Egyptians in the Red Sea, led them across Jordan's watery banks and delivered the greatest walled city, Jericho, into their hands.

At the battle of Ai, Joshua failed to unite the attention of the people against a single adversary and take care that nothing will split up that attention. Instead, Joshua allowed the spies to decide how the battle should be fought. I can only imagine that the spies who were sent to Ai came back with a report such as, "Just send a few men to take Ai. Why should we all go to fight such a small town? We're tired anyway from the big battle at Jericho."

How quickly Joshua forgot what had happened forty

years earlier when Moses sent twelve men to determine the outcome of an entire nation when he sent them to spy out the land of Canaan.

We see the same thing happening within the church. Many are able to do the work of the kingdom of God, but only a few are actively engaged in the battle. The result? The victory which should be so easily won, often escapes us.

The days of the lone ranger, superstar preacher, giving his all for God while the majority of the church sits idle on the sidelines, is over.

God is raising up an end-time army of righteous men and women who are not content to sit at home while their brothers and sisters are out doing exploits for His kingdom.

If you are to defeat your enemies, you must first understand the importance of unity. In order to secure your victory, you must stand shoulder-to-shoulder and arm-in-arm with those who are fighting the good fight of faith. As a believer, you must live in total, absolute, consecrated obedience to God's Word and walk in a spirit of unity.

When we go out to battle against our adversary, we need to do it with all the resources available to us as believers. Some of our greatest assets are the power of agreement and the power and anointing of God that is brought to bear when we operate in a spirit of unity.

The Tower of Babel

The power of unity can also be used to fight against God and His commandments. The Book of Genesis records the story of a great tower that was built when the people of the earth worked together without dispute or distraction.

> And the whole earth was of one language, and of one speech. And it came to pass, as they journeyed from the east, that they found a plain in the land of Shinar; and they dwelt there.
>
> And they said one to another, Go to, let us make brick, and burn them thoroughly. And they had brick for stone, and slime had they for mortar.
>
> And they said, Go to, let us build us a city and a tower, whose top may reach unto heaven; and let us make us a name, lest we be scattered abroad upon the face of the whole earth.
>
> And the Lord came down to see the city and the tower, which the children of men builded.
>
> And the Lord said, Behold, the people is one, and they have all one language; and this they begin to do: and now nothing will be restrained from them, which they have imagined (11:1-6).

In Genesis chapter ten, God told the people of the earth to scatter but they disobeyed Him and instead pulled together. Under the leadership of the first world dictator, Nimrod, whose name means, "we will revolt," the people congregated in Babel and proceeded to attempt to build a tower to the heavens.

God knew once the world was united that there was no end to the evil that could happen. If evil men can unite to devise their evil plans, what more could you and I do when we come into unity with the Lord's plans and purposes?

Unity Through Covenant

God is looking throughout the whole earth to show Himself strong on behalf of those who will come into unity through the covenant of His Word. The very nature of covenant involves unity or agreement. Joshua was in covenant with God because of the covenant He originally made with Abraham in the Book of Genesis.

> In the same day the Lord made a covenant with Abram, saying, Unto thy seed have I given this land, from the river of Egypt unto the great river, the river Euphrates: The Kenites, and the Kenizzites, and the Kadmonites, And the Hittites, and the Perizzites, and the Rephaims, And the Amorites, and the Canaanites, and the Girgashites, and the Jebusites (15:18-21).

All Joshua and the Israelites had to do was to stake claim to the promises of the covenant in order to possess all of the Promised Land. But somewhere along the line, Joshua and the Israelites fell into their old ways, thinking they could succeed using their own plans and methods.

They divided their ranks, leaving some to go to battle at Ai and some to stay at home.

Our Heavenly Father made the ultimate covenant between Himself and His only Son, Jesus Christ. Hebrews 6:13 says, "Because he could swear by no greater, he sware by himself."

This covenant is a perfect covenant which cannot be annulled, separated, broken, or divorced. If you are a born-again believer, you have been adopted into the family of God. However, the covenant rights and blessings that you operate in are not a result of your covenant with the Father.

The covenant you entered into was a covenant made before the foundations of the world between God and our Canaan King, Jesus Christ. It is a covenant of immense proportions! It is perfection meeting perfection!

Jesus shed His sinless, spotless blood and became the perfect sacrifice—and the eternal link between God and man. God made a covenant with His own Son so you could be a partaker in all the abundance of His kingdom!

Paul admonished believers to walk in unity when he said:

> If there be therefore any consolation in Christ, if any comfort of love, if any fellowship of the Spirit, if any bowels and mercies. Fulfill ye my joy, that ye be likeminded, having the same love, being of one accord, of one mind (Philippians 2:1, 2).

To be in one accord involves being in covenant relationship with a living God who knows how to see you through every trial and circumstance.

When you come into unity with God through the covenant He made with His Son, Jesus, then you are positioned to receive all of the blessings of that covenant. Joy, health, prosperity, peace, family salvation all belong to you.

UNITY BRINGS A MULTIPLICATION OF POWER

That's why I want to add my faith to yours through the power of the Resurrection Seed—so our effectiveness in accomplishing great things for God's kingdom can be multiplied.

You have heard the old saying 'you are only as strong as your weakest link' or 'the whole is greater than the sum of its parts'? These are actually secular ways of describing a scriptural principle. Deuteronomy chapter 32, verse 30 records these words:

> How should one chase a thousand, and two put ten thousand to flight.

There is not just addition—but multiplication—when we join our forces in faith.

In other words, when your part and my part are added together, there are more than two parts of power available to us. God Himself becomes involved with us to accomplish His will in our lives. A divine multiplication factor comes into play which places supernatural ability at our disposal.

Your Jericho may be too great for you to conquer yourself. I want you to know, I am no match for Ai on my own. But together, we can destroy every obstacle the enemy places in our paths.

Victory is assured when we stand together, march into battle together, pray together, and love one another. As we join our faith together in a covenant sealed with the blood of Jesus, we will truly possess the gates of our enemies.

Whatever you need, God has promised in the Book of Isaiah:

> So shall my word be that goeth forth out of my mouth: it shall not return unto me void, but it shall accomplish that which I please, and it shall prosper in the thing whereto I sent it (55:11).

In the midst of your greatest need, we must go to battle in unity to defeat the giants before us. As you and I come together in the spirit of agreement, I believe we are going to defeat every adversary, enter into God's abundant provision and take all of our promised harvest.

Chapter 4

BUILT FOR THE BATTLE

> Again I say unto you, that if two of you shall agree on earth as touching any thing that they shall ask, it shall be done for them of my Father which is in heaven (Matthew 18:19).

In the last chapter, I shared with you the commitment or the power of unity that was necessary for the Israelites not only to conquer the walled city of Jericho but to eventually gain the victory at Ai as well. In this chapter, I want to continue to show you how the power of agreement can produce an abundant harvest in your life, resurrect your finances, breathe new life into your marriage, and bring healing to your body.

THE POWER OF AGREEMENT

A doctor of philosophy called the power of agreement the "principle of non-summativity" because the power of agreement is this: the total is greater than the sum of its parts. In other words, one plus one does not equal two. It equals anything that you need.

> When Jesus came to the coasts of Caesarea Philippi, he asked his disciples, saying, Whom do

> men say that I the Son of man am? And they said, Some say that thou art John the Baptist: some, Elias; and others, Jeremias, or one of the prophets.
>
> He saith unto them, But whom say ye that I am? (Matthew 16:13-15).

Jesus is still asking this question of the Church today, "Who do you say that I am?"

Did you know that Jesus can only be to you who you say that He is. If you believe that He is your Savior, then that is what He will be. If you believe that the Son of God is Savior and Deliverer, then that is what He will be. If you believe that He is Savior, Healer, and Deliverer, then that is what He will be. If you believe that He is Savior, Healer, Deliver, and that it is His will to prosper you, then that is what He will be to you. In other words, anything you can believe that Jesus is that the Word says He is, and you begin to say that He is, that is exactly who He will become to you.

This passage of Scripture goes on to say: "And Simon Peter answered and said, Thou art the Christ, the Son of the living God" (vs. 16).

There were many rumors circulating around town as to the true identity of Jesus and He wanted to know what the townsfolk were saying about Him. But Peter was the only one who received the true revelation of Jesus when he acknowledged Him as the Christ—"the anointed one that destroys every yoke." (See Matthew 16:17.)

It wasn't that Jesus didn't know who He was. The reality was that Jesus was looking for someone who knew Him as the anointed One so that He could come into agreement with them.

Jesus wanted to join together the natural and the spiritual. When you understand who Jesus is, then there is hope for today and help for tomorrow. There is healing available to you for your body. Prosperity for your finances belongs to you. There is deliverance for your family because Jesus is who He said He was!

Because of the revelation Peter received, Jesus went on to say to him in the Gospel of Matthew:

> And I say also unto thee, That thou art Peter, and upon this rock I will build my church; and the gates of hell shall not prevail against it.
>
> And I will give unto thee the keys of the kingdom of heaven: and whatsoever thou shalt bind on earth shall be bound in heaven: and whatsoever thou shalt loose on earth shall be loosed in heaven (vv. 18, 19).

This is the first place Jesus mentioned His church in the New Testament. There were three specific things that the Lord mentioned in this passage. First, He said, "I will build my church." Notice, that God refers to His church as a building. A building is erected to house, or protect, something inside it—be it a family, possessions, or other valuable assets.

Second, Jesus said, "The gates of hell shall not prevail against it." Third, "I will give unto thee the keys of the kingdom of heaven."

I want to focus on the first part of this verse. As Jesus' building, the Church houses the principles of this kingdom, or God's will in the earth. God gave us His purpose, or His will. Then He set you and me in the church to fulfill that will, and to establish that purpose in the earth.

But how do we fulfill God's plan in the earth? We fulfill His purpose through the dominion we have been given in Genesis 1:26, 27:

> And God said, Let us make man in our image, after our likeness: and let them have dominion over the fish of the sea, and over the fowl of the air, and over the cattle, and over all the earth, and over every creeping thing that creepeth upon the earth. So God created man in his own image, in the image of God created he him; male and female created he them.

Along with this authority, you need the Lord's anointing because anointing is His ability manifested through your availability. When His ability begins to manifest through your availability to that anointing, then you can become the person God has established in the earth to interpret His will and purpose.

The reality is that Jesus not only died, He was resurrected from the dead and the reading of His will takes place every time you open His Word. When you break open the seals of the Bible you find out you what your inheritance is.

Third John 2 declares that part of our legacy is that, "above all things that thou mayest prosper and be in health, even as thy soul prospereth." The word "wish" in this Scripture actually means "will." God's will is your complete and total prosperity in every area of your life. He wants you to take all of the blessings that belong to you through His covenant promises as you can come into agreement with Him. God's desire is to give you anything that you want or need.

Two or Three Gathered in Jesus' Name

The passage in Matthew 16:19 directly corresponds to the verse in Matthew 18:18. "And whatsoever you bind on earth shall be bound in heaven, and whatsoever you loose on earth shall be loosed in heaven."

In the Gospel of Matthew 18:18-20, Jesus declared:

> Verily I say unto you, whatsoever ye shall bind on earth shall be bound in heaven: and whatsoever ye shall loose on earth shall be loosed in heaven. Again I say unto you, that if two of you shall agree on earth as touching any thing that they shall ask, it shall be done for them of my father which is in heaven. For where two or three are gathered together in my name, there am I in the midst of them.

In the Gospel of John, Jesus prayed that we might be one in him and in one spirit with each other. You see, God places within our hearts His desire. Then, in a spirit of agreement, we approach Him in prayer and ask Him for that desire. When we do, He answers us according to His Word. This is the essence of the spirit of unity—all of us in agreement with His Word, receiving the desires of our heart! What is the hope of your heart?

Remember, I stated earlier than one plus one equals anything you need. I believe as you grasp this revelation of agreement you will defeat every foe that stands in your way and take all of your promised harvest.

I believe 2004 truly is a prophetic year when the unity and agreement God desires for His people will be manifested. I believe this year, we will be drawn together by the Holy Spirit with one heart and one voice to exalt the Lord in our lives. When we do, absolute, overwhelming victory is assured!

The corporate anointing to propel us into the supernatural outpouring of God will come when we walk in our calling as one body. Psalm 133 says it this way:

> Behold, how good and how pleasant it is for brethren to dwell together in unity! It is like the precious ointment upon the head, that ran down upon the beard, even Aaron's beard: that went down to the skirts of his garments; as the dew of Hermon, and as the dew that descended upon the mountains of Zion: for there the Lord commanded the blessing, even life for evermore (1-3).

I am convinced we will experience an unprecedented outpouring of God's supernatural power and provision when we walk in unity. We are the generation and this is our destiny!

Unity is vital to victory in both war and peace, for a country. Our success as believers depends also upon unity —for here we find protection and provision. As I shared in the last chapter, we see this very truth played out in the life of Joshua and the Israelites. They prepared to attack Ai, following their victory at Jericho. According to Joshua 7:3, they became divided.

> And they returned to Joshua, and said unto him, let not all the people go up; but let about two or three thousand men go up and smite Ai; and make not all the people to labour thither; for they are but few.

However, Israel's problems actually began when

Achan took a Babylonian garment, some silver, and a wedge of gold from the conquest of Jericho. God had already told Israel that the spoils of that city belonged specifically to Him. The triumph of Jericho belonged to the people, but the treasure belonged to the Lord.

This one act of disobedience caused Israel to begin making one wrong decision after another. When they arrived at Ai, God left them to their own devices. He recognized that their hearts were filled with the desires found in the stolen treasure of Achan and not with His prophetic word. When people lack unity and are divided, too often it is because their hearts are following after the wrong kind of treasure.

Remember the Bible says, where your treasure is, there will your heart be also. (See Matthew 6:21.) Joshua and the children of Israel learned a hard lesson. Once again they made the choice to follow after the Lord with their whole heart and be obedient to His command. Joshua 8:1, 2 tell us:

> The Lord said unto Joshua, fear not, neither be thou dismayed: take all the people of war with thee, and arise, go up to Ai: see, I have given into thy hand the king of Ai, and his people, and his city, and his land. And thou shalt do to Ai and her king as thou didst unto Jericho and her king as thou didst unto Jericho and her king.

Joshua and the children of Israel all went forth together to defeat their common adversary.

Though we may be weak in the natural, there is a job for each of us to do. It doesn't matter what your race, gender, or age—everyone is called to be set in their own special place in the conflict.

Why is unity so important? Alone, we are no match for disease and depravity. Divided, we cannot stand against rumors of wars and downturns in the economy. But, united in the purpose and power of God, we are transformed from the conquered to the conqueror.

God's Word declares that we are more than conquerors through Jesus Christ who loves us. (See Romans 8:37.) The hour has come for the church not to backup, not to remain stagnant—but to advance. We are to move past our Jericho, subdue our enemies, and take all of the promised harvest.

This year I believe the God-ordained purpose of all who name the name of Jesus Christ as their Lord is to come together in a spirit of unity to defeat and destroy the spiritual forces attacking our families, our finances, and our future.

What was the reward promised to God's people for following His command? According to Joshua 24:13, they would possess a land overflowing with houses they didn't build and vineyards they didn't plant.

Unity is the common bond and sign of an end-time church that is completely sold out to God. There's a land of blessing, a land of healing, and a land freedom waiting for us as, together, we seize the enemies standing in the way of total victory and take all of our harvest.

Everyone attached to this ministry is connected to one another through a covenant relationship that gives them the ability to agree with somebody on earth and touch one thing and it shall be done. Because of that then, whatever you bind is bound and whatever you loose is loosed.

But we must resist the desire to give in to compromise. We must overtake our adversaries of disease, lack, defeat, and discouragement and refuse to become complacent with just a few victories in our land of promises.

Together in one Accord

The theme of unity is interwoven throughout the Bible. For example, in the Book of Acts we continually see the power of unity in the Church of Jesus Christ. Again and again believers were filled and refilled with the Holy Spirit as they were assembled together all in one accord and in one place. Acts 2:1-4 declare:

> And when the day of Pentecost was fully come, they were all with one accord in one place.
>
> And suddenly there came a sound from heaven as of a rushing mighty wind, and it filled all the house where they were sitting. And there appeared unto them cloven tongues like as of fire, and it sat upon each of them.
>
> And they were all filled with the Holy Ghost, and began to speak with other tongues, as the Spirit gave them utterance."

Again Acts 4:31, 32 also proclaim:

> And when they had prayed, the place was shaken where they were assembled together; and they were all filled with the Holy Ghost . . . And the multitude of them that believed were of one heart and of one soul.

Notice that the place was shaken where they were assembled together all with one accord and in one place and they were all filled with the Holy Spirit. Why? Because we found out earlier in Matthew eighteen that wherever two or three are gathered together in Jesus' name there He is in the midst of them.

That is the reason the Bible expressly commands us to forsake not "the assembling of ourselves together, as the manner of some is; but exhorting one another: and so much the more, as ye see the day approaching" (Hebrews 10:25).

In both Acts 2 and 4 we discover that as these believers came to together in one accord, not only were they filled with the Holy Spirit but all of their needs were met.

> Neither was there any among them that lacked; for as many as were possessors of lands or houses sold them, and brought the prices of the things that were sold, And laid them down at the apostles' feet: and distribution was made unto every man according as he had need (Acts 4:34, 35).

None of God's people lacked anything because they gave God everything. Whatever the Lord puts His hand on belongs to Him. You see every dollar that you receive belongs to God but He simply asks for the tithe and an offering so that your obedience will release His blessing. When the early Church sowed all, they could take all of the harvest that they needed.

This word of unity is like the word the Lord gave to Joshua for the children of Israel. It is a word to bring you out and take you into prosperity. If you apply this word to your finances, I believe you can leave lack behind forever.

Today, the Resurrection Seed is this ministry's greatest

symbol of unity. It is a time when everyone gathers up their seed, for many it is at least one week's income, and sows it believing for a one hundred fold return. Every year for twenty years God has honored our obedience to this word.

My Prayer of Agreement With You

Father, bless every person that reads this book. Let this be the beginning of your Church coming into one accord, to fulfill your divine command. We look forward to your commanded blessing toward us.

Right now I agree that your body is healed and that your mind is at peace. I believe with you that every principality and power is bound and that the devil has no authority in your mind, your body, your family, your finances, or your future. I give glory to God believing that your miracle harvest is already here and it is time for you to take it all. Amen.

Chapter 5

TAKE IT ALL

> Only the spoil thereof, and the cattle thereof, shall ye take for a prey unto yourselves (Joshua 8:2).

Joshua and the nation of Israel were ready to go up against the nation of Ai again. They had cleansed the camp of Achan's sin, re-committed themselves in unity to the battle and rehearsed God's commission. Now it was time to follow the command of God to take all of the harvest. God said to Joshua:

> Fear not, neither be thou dismayed: take all the people of war with thee, and arise, go up to Ai: see, I have given into thy hand the king of Ai, and his people, and his city, and his land: and thou shalt do to Ai and her king as thou didst unto Jericho and her king: only the spoil thereof, and the cattle thereof, shall ye take for a prey unto yourselves (8:1,2).

This time, the nation would not be defeated. As they pursued their promise, united in one spirit and in one purpose, their reward would be unimaginable. The result was a great shift in the wealth of this wicked city into the hands of the children of God. They were about to take it all!

Moses spoke prophetically years earlier:

> And it shall be, when the Lord thy God shall have brought thee into the land which he sware unto thy fathers, to Abraham, to Isaac, and to Jacob, to give thee great and goodly cities, which thou buildedst not, and houses full of all good things, which thou filledst not, and wells digged, which thou diggedst not, vineyards and olive trees, which thou plantedst not (Deuteronomy 6:10, 11).

God had already granted Israel the victory long before they arrived in Canaan. Just like the possessions of Canaan were transferred to the Israelites after their battle at Ai, there is about to be a tremendous transfer of wealth to this generation. Ecclesiastes 2:26 refers to this great end-time transfer of wealth:

> To the man who pleases him, God gives wisdom, knowledge and happiness, but to the sinner he gives the task of gathering and storing up wealth to hand it over to the one who pleases God (NIV).

Just as God was waiting for the Israelites to take all of their inheritance after they conquered Canaan, another man, Isaac, several years earlier sowed a seed and took all the hundredfold harvest it produced.

An Hundredfold Harvest

Isaac, second in line of Hebrew ancient patriarchs, surveyed the scene. The land was nothing more than a dry and barren wasteland, which could neither satisfy thirst nor sustain life. The land was famine-stricken.

This wasn't the first famine. Seventy-years earlier his father, Abraham, had witnessed the ravages of drought and death. Now Isaac too experienced how the once fertile soil was useless to produce a harvest.

Isaac had a choice to make. Stay where he was and hope he and his family would survive or search for a better land to sustain them. The Book of Genesis records:

> And there was a famine in the land, beside the first famine that was in the days of Abraham. And Isaac went unto Abimelech king of the Philistines unto Gerar (26:1).

Isaac and his family were facing one of the worst famines in recorded history at that time. The parched and dusty earth was ravaged by drought; there was nothing to harvest and nothing to eat. The famine was so severe that Isaac took his family and his flocks and left his homeland, in search of a better land and a better life. But along the way, the Lord apprehended Isaac. The story continues:

> And the Lord appeared unto him, and said, go not down into Egypt; dwell in the land which I shall tell thee of: sojourn in this land, and I will be with thee, and will bless thee; for unto thee, and unto thy seed, I will give all these countries, and I will perform the oath which I sware unto Abraham thy father.
>
> And I will make thy seed to multiply as the stars of heaven, and will give unto thy seed all these countries; and in thy seed shall the nations of the earth be blessed; because that Abraham obeyed my voice, and kept my charge, my commandments, my statutes, and my laws (vv. 2-5).

God's word to His servant was simply this: "Stay where you are—in the land of famine."

Faith in Times of Famine

You or I might be tempted to question whether that was really God. But the truth is that the Lord will never create a lifestyle for you in which He is unnecessary.

Our Heavenly Father's ability to bless us and provide for us isn't based upon our current circumstances. Yet too many allow what's in their cupboard or bank account to become the determining factor of defeat or victory in their lean times. Ecclesiastes 11:4 declares:

> He that observeth the wind shall not sow; and he that regardeth the clouds shall not reap.

In other words, if you are looking at your circumstances before deciding whether to obey the Bible, then you are slipping slowly backwards in the economy of God.

Faith refuses to regard the rain, but instead reaches for the rainbow. The same wind that'll stop a doubter will propel a person of faith into their destiny.

Just like Isaac, when God's word is heard, you have a decision to make: to respond in faith—or in fear. Too many of the blessings of God have been forfeited, and untold souls have been lost because believers have waited for the winds of adversity to die down before they venture forth in the plan of God.

Our Heavenly Father wants each and every one of us to move and breathe in the God-kind of faith that sees the cloud the size of a man's hand rising over the horizon full of rain for a famine-stricken land—and food on the table, the bills paid and money in the bank even when you don't have a dollar to change!

The Apostle Peter learned all too quickly what happens when we take our focus off God and place it on our circumstances. Jesus said in the Gospel of Matthew:

> But straightway Jesus spake unto them, saying, be of good cheer; it is I; be not afraid. And Peter answered him and said, Lord, if it be thou, bid me come unto thee on the water. And he said, come. And when Peter was come down out of the ship, he walked on the water, to go to Jesus. But when he saw the wind boisterous, he was afraid; and beginning to sink, he cried, saying, Lord, save me. (14:27-30).

It was faith that compelled Peter to step out of the boat. But it was fear that caused him to turn his focus to his surroundings. When the winds and waves of life rage, there is a rainbow of blessing waiting for those who will trust in God and His Word.

In the Same Year Isaac Took all of the Harvest

If you look again at the story of Isaac, you will see that he was positioned to possess the land when he obeyed the voice of the Lord and dwelt in the land of Gerar. He stayed in the land of famine and planted his seed in the parched earth. I can only imagine the faith it took to take the sustenance for his family and bury it in the dusty soil. Why, any farmer knows the folly of sowing in such conditions—

the seed would be blown away before the next sunrise!

When Isaac took a step of faith in obedience to the word of the Lord, Genesis 26:12, 13 proclaim:

> Then Isaac sowed in that land, and received in the same year an hundredfold; and the Lord blessed him. And the man waxed great, and went forward, and grew until he became very great.

Notice that this passage of Scripture says, in the same year that there was a famine in the land—in the midst of economic doom and gloom, Isaac sowed as a demonstration of his faith in God and His word—and in the same year—from one single harvest—he received a hundredfold return!

But that was only the beginning! That same verse of Scripture goes on to say that Isaac grew until he became very great!

There he set up a homestead, sowed a seed, and dug a well. In return, he reaped a one-hundred-fold return on his seed sown. He took all of the harvest.

If you are constantly monitoring the economic forecast or the mountain of bills as they seem to endlessly pile up, you will miss the provision God has prepared for you. But when you trust in God and His word and let go of what is in your hand toward Him, then He will let go of what is in His hand toward you.

God never intended for you to be bound to the fluctuations of interest rates or stock market averages. He wants you to take all of your harvest, and He has provided the principles in His Word to help you prosper.

You may be facing bankruptcy or layoff. Perhaps there is a mountain of bills that you cannot seem to overcome.

Temptation may be high to eat your seed. But without sowing, there can be no harvest.

Just like Isaac, God can cause you to prosper regardless of the economy—regardless of the fluctuations in the stock market—regardless of the balance in your bank account.

As a New Testament believer, God will do exceeding abundantly above all you can ask or think when you act in faith according to His word to you. It doesn't matter whether your checking account is zero. Right in the middle of your famine and in the middle of your greatest enemy God has already provided for your triumph.

God's Kingdom vs. the World's System

The kingdom of God is diametrically opposed to the kingdom of this world. While the world's system is rooted in greed and holding on to what you have—in God's kingdom, the way to get more is to give more. In order to have something you've never had before, you must do something you've never done before. Jesus declared in Luke 6:38:

> Give, and it shall be given unto you; good measure, pressed down, and shaken together, and running over, shall men give into your bosom. For with the same measure that ye mete withal it shall be measured to you again.

As Christians we can put our trust in a loving God who has promised to provide exceeding abundantly for us in our time of need—when we rely on Him and obey His commands.

Obedience to God's Word is not an option if you want to take all of the harvest that He has for you. The laws of sowing and reaping are true whether the economy is booming and the money's flowing or the financial water tap has run dry.

It is time for the church to turn its gaze toward heaven for its supply instead of depending on what the world has to offer. But sometimes the Lord will ask you to do something so out of the ordinary that it absolutely boggles your mind.

SEEDTIME AND HARVEST

If you want to receive a bumper crop of blessing in the lean times—God says to sow.

- Isaac sowed a crop and received an hundredfold return.
- Israel sowed all the spoils of Jericho and took all the spoils at Ai.

This is the time for God's people to stand firm in their faith without wavering. Like Isaac facing famine and drought with everyone around him speaking doom and gloom, he was ready to pack up and move on. But God's Word was simply to stay where you are.

We just need to obey the voice of the Lord and see Him move on our behalf

God wants to bless you even more than you desire to be blessed. That's why the principles of seedtime and harvest are fundamental to taking all of your harvest in times of famine as well as times of plenty. Genesis 8:22 says it this way:

> While the earth remaineth, seedtime and harvest, and cold and heat, and summer and winter, and day and night shall not cease.

God always delivers with a seed.

Maybe you are believing for a supernatural harvest in your finances. Perhaps you are struggling to make ends meet—and simple things such as school clothes for the kids or unexpected medical bills are draining your faith and causing you to fear.

I believe the Lord's prophetic word to you through this book is this: it is time to take it all. There's a harvest of blessing on the horizon of your future.

Your Future Is Subject to Change

Second Corinthians 4:18 declares:

> While we look not at the things which are seen, but at the things which are not seen: for the things which are seen are temporal; but the things which are not seen are eternal.

The word "temporal" in this passage of Scripture simply means "subject to change." That means that your financial drought is subject to change. Your endless days of famine and lack are subject to change! Your future is subject to change!

You may be thinking, "Well, you don't know what I am facing." It really doesn't matter because God's already prepared you to receive your harvest.

Whatever enemies await you the Lord wants you to dream your wildest dream. Go ahead. Take the greatest step of faith you have ever taken in your life. God is waiting to show you that He is a rewarder of those who seek Him.

Right now, you may be facing an insurmountable adversary. Perhaps it is a stronghold of unforgiveness or bitterness that has held you captive for years. Your blessings seem like they are just behind the walls of your spiritual Ai. You can see your land of promise, but a mighty fortress stands between you and your victory on the other side!

Friend, I have good Gospel news for you: just as God brought final victory to Israel at Ai, He is ready and willing to lead you into your land of promise as well.

My Prayer for You

Heavenly Father, let faith arise in the hearts of your people. Bless them with supernatural provision in their land of famine. Bare your mighty right arm against their enemies on their behalf. Let not one seed fall to the ground void of power—but let their seed burst forth exponentially and produce a hundredfold return in their lives as they possess their Promised Land and take the harvest you have already prepared for them. I believe you to do it by your grace and power. In the mighty name of Jesus Christ. Amen.

Whatever giants you may be facing today there is a fertile land of miracles waiting just for you. You too can take it all.

Chapter 6

YOUR HARVEST IS HERE

> Only the cattle and the spoil of that city Israel took for a prey unto themselves, according unto the word of the Lord which he commanded Joshua (Joshua 8:27).

I love the rolling plains of South Texas. There have been times when I visited this beautiful countryside, when my friends and I would happen among a herd of cattle. Sometimes one of the men would stop and look at one of the herd and say, "I better go put that one back." I would ask, "What do you mean?" His response, "It doesn't have our brand. It doesn't belong to us."

God has always had somebody that He has set His mark on. In 2004, it will not be hard to distinguish the believers who have given all in faith in order to walk in God's divine promises. They will have the right brand. They will be those who are not afraid to join other believers in one accord, believing the Word of the Lord for their victory.

To be a part of this remnant believers it will cost you everything. God will brand you by engraving His Word upon the fleshly tablets of your heart. What does it mean to you? It means God's Word will become a tangible part of the fabric of your life. It will not be an addendum, or an afterthought.

When you named the name of Jesus Christ, He put His brand on you. He marked you for life and said, "My purpose has now become your purpose."

God's Chosen People

The Israelites were branded as God's own "chosen" people. They were marked by circumcision, and the Lord had a purpose for them—to possess Canaan. Earlier I shared with you that as part of God's plan, Israel was directed to follow the commission of the Lord to fight Ai in a commitment to unity. We must remember that it was also a part of God's commandment to Joshua and the Israelites at the battle Jericho to maintain a "hands off" approach to the spoils of that city. Joshua 6:17 declares: "And the city shall be accursed, even it, and all that are therein, to the Lord."

God's command was "do not touch the spoils of Jericho." Why? Because Jericho was the first city to be conquered by the Israelites, and the firstfruits always belong to God. His blessings always follow your obedience to His commands.

It had to have been hard for the Israelites to stand before the wealth of Jericho and walk away. But God had already prepared the blessing for all those who heard and obeyed. When the Israelites attacked Ai, God would give them all the spoils of that city.

But one man, Achan, did not obey the command at Jericho—and jeopardized not only the blessing that had already been provided by God for the Israelites—but their very lives as well.

Achan was like the man who went to God and said, "If I had one hundred pigs, I would give you fifty." God's response was, "No, you wouldn't. You have two pigs and you won't give me one."

When you stretch forth your hand to use what God has sanctified for Himself, you step outside the realm of His protection and provision. The river of divine flow into your life begins to dries up.

The same is true regarding our tithes and offerings unto the Lord. Let's look at a familiar passage found in Malachi 3:10:

> Bring ye all the tithes into the storehouse, that there may be meat in mine house, and prove me now herewith, saith the Lord of hosts, if I will not open you the windows of heaven, and pour you out a blessing, that there shall not be room enough to receive it.

When you sanctify, or set aside, all of your tithe unto the Lord, He is faithful to pour out more than enough blessing for you to receive. But sometimes the Word of the Lord goes contrary to everything we have been taught.

Victory at Jericho

Let's look again at what happened at the battle of Jericho. Joshua gave the children of Israel God's instructions: march six days around the walled city and leave their weapons at home. That was a strange word. The fact is, however, that the command of God rarely, if ever, makes sense to your natural mind. Why? Because once a

Word is given faith—not reason—is demanded.

I am sure to the inhabitants of Jericho, the Israelites looked foolish marching around the greatest walled city of Canaan without a weapon among them. But always remember, even though your adversary mocks you and laughs you to shame, just keep your head down and keep marching. It may seem like you against the world. You may feel like Charlie Brown, saying to yourself, "why is everybody always picking on me?" But always remember Jesus' words in Mark 11:22-24:

> Have faith in God. For verily I say unto you, That whosoever shall say unto this mountain, Be thou removed, and be thou cast into the sea; and shall not doubt in his heart, but shall believe that those things which he saith shall come to pass; he shall have whatsoever he saith.
>
> Therefore I say unto you, What things soever ye desire, when ye pray, believe that ye receive them, and ye shall have them.

In this end time God is raising up a remnant who will not be denied their position of opportunity to take all of their harvest. What is the adversary going to do with a group of people who understand if they don't have their miracle now, it means absolutely nothing! God promises that you shall have it! So when the devil tries to tell you that you're never going to get that job, receive that healing, or see that loved one saved, know that our Commander in Chief, Jesus Christ, is leading the charge and you shall have it. When your husband says he is leaving, just keep marching. When the Dow Jones takes a nose dive, just keep marching. The truth is, that you have come too far to turn back now.

The Israelites were to march for six days. On the seventh day, God changed His instructions. The children of God were to march seven times around Jericho and on the last march they were to raise up a shout of victory. The Israelites were obedient to do as God commanded. As their victory shouts filled the air—God took over. Jericho imploded before their very eyes and the greatest walled city became nothing but a pile of rubble.

Are you convinced that you can't do anything about the fortress walls that are surrounding you? Do you declare before God that with Him all things are possible, and without Him nothing is possible? Are you ready to make that confession before God?

Jesus Christ, the Seed of David

In order to truly understand that God wants us to take all of our harvest in this final hour we must receive the revelation that Jesus is the living seed of the Word.

Look at the words recorded in Acts 2:22-25:

> Ye men of Israel, hear these words; Jesus of Nazareth, a man approved of God among you by miracles and wonders and signs, which God did by him in the midst of you, as ye yourselves also know: Him, being delivered by the determinate counsel and foreknowledge of God, ye have taken, and by wicked hands have crucified and slain: Whom God hath raised up, having loosed the pains of death: because it was not possible that he should

> be holden of it. For David speaketh concerning him, I foresaw the Lord always before my face, for he is on my right hand, that I should not be moved.

Compare this to 2 Timothy 2:7-9:

> Consider what I say; and the Lord give thee understanding in all things. Remember that Jesus Christ of the seed of David was raised from the dead according to my gospel: Wherein I suffer trouble as an evil doer, even unto bonds; but the word of God is not bound.

From reading these two passages of Scripture, you understand that Jesus came out of the lineage of David, and is rightly called the seed of David. Another definition for seed is "word." John declared that in the beginning was the word and the word was with God and the word was God. (See John 1:1.) Jesus is the living word. This is a critical point I do not want you to miss. David said it was not possible that death should hold Him. Why? Because He is the living Word of God.

What made a dead Jesus live again? The seed of the Word. Death could not hold Him anymore than the spirit of lack can hold up the great transfer of wealth from the hands of the wicked God has provided for you. Death could not hold Him anymore than sickness can hold onto your body. Death could not hold Him anymore than divorce can hold onto your life when you get a word from the Lord! It was a prophetic word spoken by men such as David and the prophet Isaiah that hundreds of years earlier invaded the borrowed tomb of Joseph of Arimathaea, and raised to life again the three-day-dead body of the Prince of God!

Because Jesus was raised from the dead, we have now become children of the King of Kings and Lord of Lords, and we have an inheritance. The Book of Romans says it this way:

> The Spirit itself beareth witness with our spirit, that we are the children of God: And if children, then heirs; heirs of God, and joint-heirs with Christ; if so be that we suffer with him, that we may be also glorified together (8:16, 17).

Jesus Christ's royal blood flows through our veins. Your harvest of healing, victory, deliverance, and hope has nothing to do with your merit, and everything to do with His mercy. It has nothing to do with your goodness, and everything to do with His grace. It is for Christ's sake that He has redeemed us.

The Ultimate Seed Gives us the Ultimate Victory

When the season of spring approaches, the evidence of new life can be found all around. Blades of grass pushing up through the last winter's snow, birds singing in the trees as they watch over their nests, and flowers emerging from their wintry sleep.

Just when you think that there is no life to be found, the seeds that were planted months before, spring forth to life.

It only takes one seed to produce an amazing harvest. When you sow it, for awhile it may seem as if it has died. But what you don't know is that your seed has simply been waiting for the right conditions to present themselves to burst forth to life.

It is our mandate, our reasonable service, and divine call to direct people to the ultimate Seed of all protection and provision, Jesus Christ! He gave His all on Calvary so that you and I could take all of God's blessings for our own. The truth is, the war has already been won. On Calvary's hill thousands of years ago, one who was born a man, yet completely God, gave His all on an old rugged cross. He sowed the ultimate seed, His own life, so we could take it—all of the healing, all of the abundance, all of the joy, all of the blessing, all of the anointing—all!

What are those blessings that are a part of our inheritance? What are some of the benefits we can reap as a result of this one Seed? Healing is the children's bread. First Peter 2:24 declares,

> Who his own self bare our sins in his own body on the tree, that we, being dead to sins, should live unto righteousness: by whose `stripes ye were healed.

Deliverance belongs to us according to the words of Jesus in the Gospel of Luke 4:18, 19:

> The Spirit of the Lord is upon me, because he hath anointed me to preach the gospel to the poor; he hath sent me to heal the brokenhearted, to preach deliverance to the captives, and recovering of sight to the blind, to set at liberty them that are bruised, To preach the acceptable year of the Lord.

The ultimate seed opened the windows to the ultimate harvest of prosperity. Third John 2 states:

> Beloved, I wish above all things that thou mayest prosper and be in health, even as thy soul prospereth.

Because of the seed of Jesus, household salvation is our promise too.

> Believe on the Lord Jesus Christ, and thou shalt be saved, and thy house (Acts 16:31).

Freedom requires sacrifice on our part. Israel made a sacrifice at Jericho of all the spoils. Christ made the ultimate sacrifice upon the Cross. One time a year during Resurrection Seed, we give our greatest sacrifice so that we might take all of the harvest.

I believe there is a remnant of believers rising above the attack of the enemy as the Church of Jesus Christ takes its rightful place as the agent of change in this world. Satan may be the prince and power of the air, but we have been promised dominion in the earth, and the time has come for the Church to stand up and tell the devil to get his hands off our harvest of health, dominion, power, victory, our family, and deliverance!

We have received our marching orders—to take all of the spoils of this war. It's not an option for those who name the name of Jesus Christ. We are marked, consecrated, and set apart as a peculiar people and holy nation of believers!

I believe with all my heart that God is calling His people to advance like a mighty army in this end-time hour to fight the good fight of faith and reap a harvest about which we have only dreamed. He has given us powerful weapons to help us every step of the way. "For the weapons of our warfare are not carnal, but mighty through God to the pulling down of strongholds" (2 Corinthians 10:4).

I Lend you my Sword

Throughout the years, Christians have gained a reputation as soldiers of the cross. Today we need to continue the fight and do whatever is necessary to bring the revelation of prosperity to the Church and the world. Our act of giving should be a natural outgrowth of the love of God birthed in us by the complete sacrifice of a Savior who came from a limitless heaven to give us all the benefits of the kingdom.

Everywhere you look, Jesus Christ is moving through the darkness onto center stage. There is a battle going on and we need to lend one another our swords. As believers in Jesus Christ, we are all part of the arm of the Lord and we are all in the battle together. Alone we are no match for the enemy, but together we are a mighty force for the Kingdom. That's why the Book of Acts says:

> And all that believed were together, and had all things common: And sold their possessions and goods, and parted them to all men, as every man had need (2:44, 45).

God is a God of more than enough. He wants us to take all of our harvest, so we will have more than enough left over to provide for those in need.

God has promised in His Word, that whatever you make happen in another's life, He will make happen in your life as well. I firmly believe that we are positioned for the greatest end-time harvest the world has ever known. But we must continue to give, to sow, to drive out the enemies in our Promised Land until Jesus returns and reap the harvest, which awaits us. It is time to take it all!

Conclusion

PLANT YOUR VICTORY FLAG

Jesus conquered Satan on the cross of Calvary, and now we have been commanded to enforce His glorious victory.

Now it is time for you and me to route the enemy and enforce the boundaries of God's kingdom. Your harvest is here and it is time to take back your home, your joy, your provision, your peace, your health, and your prosperity. We have crossed into our Land of Promise and faced our greatest enemies. Now we must possess our harvest and take it all for God's glory.

We have taken on the enemies of God, wrestling not against flesh and blood, but against principalities, powers, the rulers of the darkness of this world, and spiritual wickedness in high places (Ephesians 6:12). His enemies have become our enemies.

Jesus has given us a new set of armor and powerful weapons to stand against the forces of darkness and has given us a mandate to take His weapons and go into battle It is time to take the high ground of victory in your home, your body, your finances, your future! Plant your victory flag, square your shoulders, run to the battle, and take all of your harvest.

Out of the ashes of yesterday's church, I believe God is raising up a whole new kind of believer—one which the devil has never had to deal with before.

They are the Elishas and the Elijahs. They are the Shadrachs, the Meschachs, the Abednegos, and the Daniels. They are those who refuse to bow and could not burn—a people within a people, a man in a family, a church in a city —not everybody—somebody.

My question to you is simply this: why not you—why not now? There is a battalion barricaded behind the walls of your Ai, and it is time to go on the offensive and take it all.

My Prayer for You

God, I pray that you will baptize us in Your authority, in Your anointing, in Your ability, in Your acceptance, and that we will understand that wherever we go, You go before us.

As we go to battle against the forces of darkness, You have already commanded us through a prophetic word to take all of the spoils of victory—healing, salvation, and glorious freedom. We thank You that as we are obedient to Your commands, we will be blessed coming in and blessing going out. Our children will be blessed. They will rise up and call us blessed. Everything that we set our hand to shall prosper.

Meet every need of every Partner and friend of this ministry, that there is nothing to hinder us from fulfilling Your purpose. For this, we seek healing for our bodies, that You may use us. We ask clarity of mind and strength of stature, that You might use us for your glory. Give us the power to get wealth according to Your Word, that we might establish Your kingdom in the earth and bring our precious

Savior, the Lamb of God slain from the foundation of the world, the rewards of His suffering—the crown jewel of souls.

There is no sacrifice too great, no duty too small for You who gave Your all on a cruel rugged cross all mankind. grant us the grace and power to give our all as we invade enemy-held territory and take it all for Your glory! In Jesus' name we pray. Amen.

SCRIPTURES

While the earth remaineth, seedtime and harvest, and cold and heat, and summer and winter, and day and night shall not cease (Genesis 8:22).

In blessing I will bless thee, and in multiplying I will multiply thy seed as the stars of the heaven, and as the sand which is upon the sea shore; and thy seed shall possess the gate of his enemies; And in thy seed shall all the nations of the earth be blessed; because thou hast obeyed my voice (Genesis 22:17, 18).

Then Isaac sowed in that land, and received in the same year an hundredfold; and the Lord blessed him. And the man waxed great, and went forward, and grew until he became very great (Genesis 26:12, 13).

And Moses sent them to spy out the land of Canaan, and said unto them, Get you up this way southward, and go up into the mountain: And see the land, what it is; and the people that dwelleth therein, whether they be strong or weak, few or many. And be ye of good courage, and bring of the fruit of the land. Now the time was the time of the firstripe grapes (Numbers 13:17, 18 and 20b).

And it shall be, when the Lord thy God shall have brought thee into the land which he sware unto thy fathers, to Abraham, to Isaac, and to Jacob, to give thee great and goodly cities, which thou buildedst not, and houses full of all good things, which thou filledst not, and wells digged, which thou diggedst not, vineyards and olive trees, which thou plantedst not (Deuteronomy 6:10, 11).

For the Lord thy God bringeth thee into a good land, in a land of brooks of water, of fountains and depths that spring out of valleys and hills; A land of wheat, and barley, and vines, and fig trees, and pomegranates; a land of oil olive, and honey; A land wherein thou shalt eat bread without scarceness, thou shalt not lack any thing in it; a land whose stones are iron, and out of whose hills thou mayest dig brass. When thou hast eaten and art full, then thou shat bless the LORD thy God for the good land which he hath given thee (Deuteronomy 8:7-10).

But thou shalt remember the Lord thy God: for it is he that giveth thee power to get wealth, that he may establish his covenant which he sware unto thy fathers, as it is this day (Deuteronomy 8:18)..

How should one chase a thousand, and two put ten thousand to flight (Deuteronomy 32:30).

Moses my servant is dead; now therefore arise, go over this Jordan, thou, and all this people, unto the land which I do give to them, even to the children of Israel Every place that the sole of your foot shall tread upon, that have I given unto you, as I said unto Moses (Joshua 1:2, 3).

Be strong and of a good courage: for unto this people shalt thou divide for an inheritance the land, which I sware unto their fathers to give them (Joshua 1:6)

And Joshua said, Hereby ye shall know that the living God is among you, and that he will without fail drive out from before you the Canaanites, and the Hittites, and the Hivites, and the Perizzites, and the Girgashites, and the Amorites, and the Jebusites (Joshua 3:10).

And the Lord said unto Joshua, Fear not, neither be thou dismayed: take all the people of war with thee, and arise, go up to Ai: see, I have given into thy hand the king of Ai, and his people, and his city, and his land: and thou shalt do to Ai and her king as thou didst unto Jericho and her king: only the spoil thereof, and the cattle thereof, shall ye take for a prey unto yourselves (Joshua 8:1, 2).

Only the cattle and the spoil of that city Israel took for a prey unto themselves, according unto the word of the Lord which he commanded Joshua (Joshua 8:27).

Believe in the Lord your God, so shall ye be established; believe his prophets, so shall ye prosper (2 Chronicles 20:20b).

Behold, how good and how pleasant it is for brethren to dwell together in unity! It is like the precious ointment upon the head, that ran down upon the beard, even Aaron's beard: that went down to the skirts of his garments; as the dew of Hermon, and as the dew that descended upon the mountains of Zion: for there the Lord commanded the blessing, even life for evermore (Psalm 133:1-3).

Where there is no vision, the people perish: but he that keepeth the law, happy is he (Proverbs 29:18).

To the man who pleases him, God gives wisdom, knowledge and happiness, but to the sinner he gives the task of gathering and storing up wealth to hand it over to the one who pleases God (Ecclesiastes 2:26 NIV).

He that observeth the wind shall not sow; and he that regardeth the clouds shall not reap (Ecclesiastes 11:4).

So shall my word be that goeth forth out of my mouth: it shall not return unto me void, but it shall accomplish that which I please, and it shall prosper in the thing whereto I sent it (Isaiah 55:11).

Bring ye all the tithes into the storehouse, that there may be meat in mine house, and prove me now herewith, saith the Lord of hosts, if I will not open you the windows of heaven, and pour you out a blessing, that there shall not be room enough to receive it (Malachi 3:10).

Verily I say unto you, whatsoever ye shall bind on earth shall be bound in heaven: and whatsoever ye shall loose on earth shall be loosed in heaven. Again I say unto you, that if two of you shall agree on earth as touching any thing that they shall ask, it shall be done for them of my father which is in heaven. For where two or three are gathered together in my name, there am I in the midst of them (Matthew 18:18-20).

Have faith in God. For verily I say unto you, That whosoever shall say unto this mountain, Be thou removed, and be thou cast into the sea; and shall not doubt in his heart, but shall believe that those things which he saith shall come to pass; he shall have whatsoever he saith. Therefore I say unto you, What things soever ye desire, when ye pray, believe that ye receive them, and ye shall have them (Mark 11:22-24).

The Spirit of the Lord is upon me, because he hath anointed me to preach the gospel to the poor; he hath sent me to heal the brokenhearted, to preach deliverance to the captives, and recovering of sight to the blind, to set at liberty them that are bruised, To preach the acceptable year of the Lord (Luke 4:18, 19).

Give, and it shall be given unto you; good measure, pressed down, and shaken together, and running over, shall men give into your bosom. For with the same measure that ye mete withal it shall be measured to you again (Luke 6:38).

The thief cometh not, but for to steal, and to kill, and to destroy: I am come that they might have life, and that they might have it more abundantly (John 10:10).

And all that believers were together, and had all things common: And sold their possessions and goods, and parted them to all men, as every man had need (Acts 2:44, 45).

Neither was there any among them that lacked: for as many as were possessors of lands or houses sold them, and brought the prices of the things that were sold, And laid them down at the apostles' feet: and distribution was made unto every man according as he had need (Acts 4:34, 35).

Believe on the Lord Jesus Christ, and thou shalt be saved, and thy house (Acts 16:31).

The Spirit itself beareth witness with our spirit, that we are the children of God: And if children, then heirs; heirs of God, and joint-heirs with Christ; is so be that we suffer with him, that we may be also glorified together (Romans 8:16, 17).

For all the promises of God in him are yea, and in him Amen, unto the glory of God by us (2 Corinthians 1:20).

While we look not at the things which are seen, but at the things which are not seen: for the things which are seen are temporal; but the things which are not seen are eternal (2 Corinthians 4:18).

For the weapons of our warfare are not carnal, but mighty through God to the pulling down of strongholds (2 Corinthians 10:4).

For whatsoever is born of God overcometh the world: and this is the victory that overcometh the world, even our faith (1 John 5:4).

Beloved, I wish above all things that thou mayest prosper and be in health, even as thy soul prospereth (3 John 2).

ABOUT THE AUTHOR

Rod Parsley is pastor of World Harvest Church in Columbus, Ohio, a dynamic megachurch with more than 12,000 in attendance weekly.

He is also a highly sought-after crusade and conference speaker who delivers a life-changing message to raise the standards of physical purity, moral integrity, and spiritual intensity.

Parsley also hosts Breakthrough, a daily and weekly television broadcast, seen by millions across America and around the world, as well as oversees Bridge of Hope Missions and Outreach, World Harvest Bible College and Harvest Preparatory School.

He and his wife, Joni, have two children, Ashton and Austin.

OTHER BOOKS BY ROD PARSLEY

At The Cross, Where Healing Begins

Ancient Wells, Living Water

Could It Be?

Daily Breakthroughs

The Day Before Eternity

He Came First

No Dry Season (Bestseller)

No More Crumbs (Bestseller)

On the Brink (#1 Bestseller)

Repairers of the Breach

For more information about Breakthrough,
World Harvest Church,
World Harvest Bible College,
Harvest Preparatory School,
or to receive a product list of the many books,
audio and video tapes by
Rod Parsley, write or call:

Breakthrough
P.O. Box 32932
Columbus, OH 43232-0932
(614) 837-1990 (Office)

World Harvest Bible College
P.O. Box 32901
Columbus, OH 43232-0901
(614) 837-4088
www.worldharvestbiblecollege.org

Harvest Preparatory School
P.O. Box 32903
Columbus, OH 43232-0903
(614) 837-1990
www.harvestprep.org

If you need prayer, Breakthrough Prayer Warriors
are ready to pray with you
24 hours a day, 7 days a week at:
(888) 534-3838

NOTES